Original title:
Leaves in the Light

Copyright © 2025 Creative Arts Management OÜ
All rights reserved.

Author: Elliot Harrison
ISBN HARDBACK: 978-1-80581-942-4
ISBN PAPERBACK: 978-1-80581-469-6
ISBN EBOOK: 978-1-80581-942-4

Whispers of Autumn's Glow

In the breeze, they dance and swirl,
Tiny hats for squirrels that twirl.
With a crackle, pop, they hit the ground,
As critters giggle in leafy surround.

They twitched and rustled, what a sight,
Playing tag in the warm daylight.
But oh! A gust sent one for a flight,
While birds laughed low, what pure delight!

Sunlit Petals Adrift

Petals float like fuzzy boats,
Sailing soft in chubby coats.
A tiny worm peeks from below,
Says, "I hope it doesn't snow!"

Caterpillars spin in endless cheer,
Throwing parties without fear.
With tiny hats and broomsticks made,
They glide and slide, a leafy parade!

Golden Canopy Serenade

Above, a symphony of gold,
Singing songs of tales untold.
A branch swings low, a feather's jest,
"Catch me if you can!" it suggests.

A cheeky acorn tumbles down,
Bouncing off a sleepy crown.
Squirrels giggle, "Oh what fun!",
Playing tag till day is done!

Shimmers Through the Branches

Glimmers crisp like candy dreams,
More tangled than a child's schemes.
A giggle slips from bark so wise,
"Watch your head!" A nut flies by!

Chirping crickets join the show,
While lazy bees take it slow.
In this crazy, bustling hive,
Nature bursts with giggles alive!

Shadows Painted in Warmth

Underneath the branches wide,
Laughter trips with joy inside.
Sunbeams dance, a playful tease,
While squirrels fool around with ease.

Beneath their shade, the world slows down,
A creature dons a leafy crown.
Chasing shadows, giggles bloom,
As nature's comedy finds room.

Embrace of Sunlit Foliage

Bright hats made of green and gold,
Worn by critters, brave and bold.
The air is filled with rustling cheer,
Nature's jokes we long to hear.

Bouncing rays and wobbly bugs,
Tickling trees with funny hugs.
Wings flutter like giggles in flight,
Oh, the joy of such delight!

Flickering Gold Between the Trees

A sunbeam slips, a squirrel slips too,
Jokes exchanged in a radiant view.
In this glow of shimmering fun,
The whispers of mischief have begun.

Flickering shades with a hearty grin,
Nature's whimsy wrapped in skin.
Bumbling bees dance in a blur,
While flowers giggle with a stir!

Kaleidoscope of Nature's Embrace

Colors swirl, a jolly spree,
With frolicking critters, wild and free.
The art of play hangs in the air,
Like a painter's brush, without a care.

Frisking about, the shadows play,
In nature's fun, we love to stay.
Every twist brings a chuckling thrill,
As joy blooms under each green hill.

Gentle Hues of a Dimming Day

As shadows stretch their tiny feet,
The sun giggles, no sign of defeat.
Birds wear hats, quite silly indeed,
While squirrels play tag, oh what a heed!

The clouds waltz in their fluffy clothes,
Tickled by winds, it's nature that glows.
A dance of color, a laugh in the sky,
"Oh look!" they shout, "A butterfly!"

Sunbeams Entwined with Nature's Tresses

Sunlit strands in wild, giddy curls,
Nature's way of teasing the world.
A leaf with sunglasses, soaking rays,
While beetles burst into funky parades!

Breeze tickles petals, a chuckle so sweet,
They dance to music on tiny feet.
Flowers gossip under azure tones,
"Oh, what a day! We're in our zones!"

Fading Glory Under the Sun

Golden hues start to fade and play,
"Catch me if you can!" they seem to say.
A funny fox, with a twirl, does prance,
While shadows join in a silly dance!

Chasing clouds that float like dreams,
Nature giggles, or so it seems.
As critters hum, and whistle along,
Playing their part in the day's sweet song.

The Whisper of Colors in the Breeze

Colors whisper secrets to the trees,
"Tell me more!" says the buzzing bee.
A bashful bloom peeks out to tease,
While ants tell jokes that bring them to knees!

With every rustle, a chuckle bursts,
The world spins in funny, vibrant bursts.
Oh, what a sight, the giggles around,
In a silly show with nature unbound!

Autumn's Embrace in Luminous Tones

Crisp air brings giggles galore,
As colors swirl, we dance and roar.
Squirrels play tag with acorn hats,
While pumpkins smile, oh how they chat!

The sky's a canvas, painted red,
As we leap in joy, no thoughts of bed.
The harvest moon winks, quite the tease,
Amidst the crunch of autumn leaves!

The Magic Within the Arboreal Realm

In the trees, odd shapes appear,
A wizard's hat, a gnome so near.
Mushrooms giggle like little clowns,
With round red noses and polka dot gowns!

Branches wave, 'Come join the fun!'
As critters frolic, each a pun.
Bouncing nuts drop like silly bombs,
Reminding us to keep our charms!

Silhouettes of Serenity at Sundown

When shadows stretch and tickle trees,
 We chuckle softly in the breeze.
A cat named Whiskers climbs the wall,
Attempting trips through autumn's hall.

With glowing stars that wink and blurt,
 We glimpse the moon in pajama shirt.
 As night creeps in, we laugh aloud,
  Our funny tales of whimsy proud!

Glazed Treasures of the Woodland

Dewdrops sparkle like disco balls,
While critters groove down grassy halls.
A hedgehog jives, a turtle spins,
Nature's party starts, let fun begin!

Beneath the mist, we hide and peek,
As woodpeckers rap their funny beat.
With twigs in tail, a chipmunk jives,
Who knew the wild held such crazy lives!

Embracing the Golden Hour

The sun does dance, oh what a sight,
It tickles trees with warm delight.
Squirrels wear shades, oh so cool,
Playing hide and seek, what a silly fool!

Butterflies giggle, fluttering around,
While ants do a conga, not making a sound.
The flowers wink, oh what a tease,
As bees buzz by, with utmost ease.

When Nature Wears Its Crown

The branches wear crowns of golden hue,
As sunlight peeks through, just like a cue.
Birds argue closely, who sings the best,
While a lazy lizard takes a sunbathing rest!

A raccoon in shades calls it a day,
While squirrels strut in a Broadway play.
Nature's fashion show, oh what a sight,
Each critter a model, in pure daylight!

Echoes of a Sun-Drenched Path

The pebbles giggle when you tread lightly,
Tickled by rays, they shine so brightly.
Flowers make jokes, tall tales to share,
While a snail tells stories, without a care!

Sunbeams chase shadows, a silly race,
While worms giggle, wiggling with grace.
Nature's pathway twinkles and glows,
Every step you take, the laughter grows!

The Lullaby of Rustling Canopies

The trees sway gently, a soft lullaby,
While breeze joins in, as it passes by.
Critters chuckle in a leafy embrace,
As squirrels do cartwheels in this lively space.

A raccoon at the top, oh what a view,
Watching the world while munching on goo.
Nature's symphony, a playful tease,
In this light-hearted dance among the trees!

Soft Hues of a Winding Journey

Bright colors twirl on the breeze,
A butterfly flies with such ease,
It mocks my shoes, all scuffed and old,
While I search for treasures untold.

A squirrel on a branch gives a stare,
I wonder if he thinks I care,
He scampers off with a nut in tow,
As I tumble down, oh, what a show!

The sunlight glints on a puddle near,
I splash around, oh what a cheer!
With every hop, a giggle escapes,
As my pants look like silly drapes.

So here's to walks with a funny twist,
Where nature's quirks cannot be missed,
In winding paths, we laugh and play,
Chasing colors at the end of the day.

The Dance of Time in Nature's Glow

A toad croaks tunes in a leafy band,
As crickets join with a clap of a hand,
I tap my feet, but they dance away,
What's a human to do but sway?

The sun dips low, casting shadows tall,
A raccoon steals snacks, oh, the gall!
With mischief in its tiny eyes,
It waves goodbye with a cheeky sigh.

Time waddles along, very slow and grand,
A turtle creeps forth to lend a hand,
But I'm in a hurry, much to my dread,
I trip on a root, now bruised on my head!

So let's cheer for nature's quirky beat,
As creatures dance and shuffle their feet,
In the glow of dusk, laughter takes flight,
Every moment's a joy, what a humorous sight!

Fragmented Light Through Fragrant Halls

In gardens where flowers paint the scene,
A bumblebee buzzes, a tiny machine,
It lands on my nose and goes to town,
With pollen party, I wear a crown!

The sun peeks through in shimmery beams,
As I chase shadows in whimsical dreams,
But I squash a bug, oh what a plight,
In this fragrant hall, things don't feel right!

A ladybug winks, oh she's quite sly,
She rolls her eyes as I stagger by,
"Don't mind me," I shout, "just having a spree,"
She flies off laughing, a queen so free.

So here's to the wonders that make us grin,
As nature twirls and lets the fun begin,
In fragmented light where laughter reigns,
We find the joy in all its quirky gains.

Sunlit Harmony in Verdant Realms

In the park, the birds all dance,
Beneath the sun, they take a chance.
Worms in tuxedos wiggle along,
While squirrels hold a acorn song.

Butterflies play hide-and-seek,
Chasing shadows, oh, what a cheek!
A ladybug in high-heeled shoes,
Shimmies past with fancy moves.

The trees gossip, sharing a laugh,
As branches wave like a bubbly staff.
Flowers chuckle, their colors bright,
Under the fun, twinkling light.

A Canvas of Nature's Caress

The daisies wear their fancy hats,
While rabbits chat with clever spats.
A peacock struts, he's quite the show,
With friends who follow, all in tow.

The clouds take bets on who can play,
A game of tag, hip-hip-hooray!
The sun gives gold to every bloom,
While bees declare their sweet perfume.

Drifting kites paint the azure sky,
With dreams of flying oh so high.
Laughter echoes in that warm embrace,
Nature's canvas, a silly place.

Whispers Through the Canopy

The rustling leaves, a gossiping crew,
Sharing secrets, just us two.
A squirrel in shades telling tall tales,
As the wind joins in with playful gales.

The ferns gossip, 'What's the news?'
In a dress of green, they can't refuse.
A dragonfly zooms with style and flair,
Chasing a beetle, unaware of care.

The sun peeks through, golden and sly,
Tickling branches that wave hi!
The chatter grows, a hilarious buzz,
In the shade, all just because.

Golden Hues of Autumn

The trees don their brightest suits,
While pumpkins wear their shiny boots.
A hedgehog rolls in leaves piled high,
Rolling 'round like a furry pie.

The acorns play hide and seek,
While owls chuckle, 'Let's not peek!'
A fox in red joins the parade,
Suggesting a funny leaf charade.

Silly critters dance in a line,
Underneath the crisp, bright vine.
With a giggle and a playful prance,
Autumn's humor leads the dance.

Harmonies of Gold and Green

Tiny ticks in plaid jump
Swaying where the sun does prance.
Whispering giggles from the trunk,
Nature's version of a dance.

Rusty rustles up above,
A squirrel wearing shades with flair.
It's a fashion show, my love,
Nature's catwalk in the air.

The trees throw shade, oh what a jest,
With branches waving, having fun.
They know how to keep things fresh,
Especially when hosting the sun.

Giggling stems with secrets shared,
Each gust of wind a playful tease.
Nature's antics fully bared,
Creating laughter in the breeze.

Woodland Reflections at Dusk

Bouncing critters on the run,
Chasing shadows, what a sight!
Chortling frogs who laugh at puns,
In the glow of fading light.

The owls twist in silly poses,
Lint-covered friends near fuzzy bushes.
Each surprised face that reposes,
Like they just heard the best of hushes.

A hedgehog rolls like it's a game,
Wobbling down a winding road.
It's hard to show who's more to blame,
When all seem trapped in giggles mode.

Rabbits prancing like they know
What mischief lies around the bend.
A woodland circus all aglow,
With laughter echoing 'til the end.

Drifting Through the Arboreal Glow

Wobbling branches, bright and bold,
Tickle your nose with golden cheer.
Bumblebees buzz tales retold,
Every note with laughter clear.

Silly shades on bark wear smiles,
Mimicking hats from a thrift store.
Carriers of joy for miles,
Nature's jesters always score.

The breeze must think it's quite the hoot,
Juggling nutty thoughts that fly.
Can you spot the goofy root?
Always aiming for the sky.

Fluffy clouds drift by with glee,
Making faces just for fun.
In the canopy, hearts agree,
The best moments weigh a ton.

Murmurs of Joy in Every Shade

Colors blend in a raucous cheer,
Talking trees share whispers bright.
Their secrets float, a giggly sphere,
   Swirling gifts of pure delight.

Bouncing sprites with tiny feet,
They skitter, laugh, and leap around.
In every nook, a funny greet,
Like secrets traded underground.

Taunting shadows make me shake,
   Poking fun at sunny spots.
While ferns giggle and half awake,
Stealing joy from tangled knots.

In this haven, whimsy shines,
Each little laugh a gentle twist.
Nature's humor intertwines,
Creating joys you can't resist.

Glimmers Between the Boughs

In the trees where the squirrels dance,
Tiny twinkles, a shimmering chance.
Mocking shadows, they prance and tease,
Sipping sunlight like bees with ease.

Chasing the breeze, they spin and twirl,
Giggles of nature in a leafy whirl.
Pine cones tumble, a feathery fight,
Laughter erupts at the silliest sight.

A robust acorn dons a tiny hat,
Sassy little critters engage in chat.
Whispering secrets in hush and thrill,
Their leafy hideout, a comedic thrill.

Each rustle is like a ticklish tease,
Dancing green fluff in the cool, crisp breeze.
Nature's stage, both charming and bright,
With a warm wink from the sun, oh what a sight!

Radiant Cascades of Color

A sprinkle of green in a patch of gold,
Tickling tones daring to be bold.
Scarlet giggles in the amber haze,
A splash of whimsy the forest plays.

Grape purple pop, like jellybeans,
Swirling like candy in joyous themes.
Chasing each other, a frenzy so sweet,
Dancing in circles with slippery feet.

Comedic chaos as colors collide,
An array of mischief, taking a ride.
Twisting and turning in fun-laden glee,
A cartoonish riot, oh can't you see?

As the sun smiles down on the merry scene,
Nature's palette boasts bright, vivid sheen.
In the end, with a raucous delight,
Harmony blooms, oh! What a sight!

The Language of Falling Dreams

Whispered giggles as dreams take flight,
Cannonballing down, a crispy delight.
Twisting and tumbling from branches so high,
A playful plunge, like pies in the sky.

Swooshing and swooping, they land with a splash,
Creating a carpet in a colorful clash.
Delighted mischief, a whimsical tease,
In their soft landing, they dance with the breeze.

The pathway's a canvas where children frolic,
Dreams painting giggles, so bright and symbolic.
Cartwheeling joy in a shimmering spree,
As they gather 'round, playful and free.

With each gentle drop, a story unfolds,
Tales filled with laughter, in shades like golds.
Falling like feathers, dreams take their claim,
In this merry moment, we're all made the same!

Prismed Greenery in Twilight

Glowing greens in the evening sway,
As the sun waves goodbye, in a jolly way.
A comical blush on the branches above,
Giving a wink from the earth, how they shove.

Twirling and twisting, the shadows play,
Bumbling together, at the end of the day.
Chasing fireflies with a flutter of cheer,
Nature's own dance, it's perfectly clear.

With a flick and a flap, they burst into fits,
Squeaky laughter that seldom quits.
The end of the day, in a burst of delight,
Is just nature's way of keeping it light.

In the twilight glow, with a shimmer so grand,
The world gets tickled by the sun's gentle hand.
So here in the evening, with silliness rife,
We'll giggle and chuckle—it's the dance of life!

Nature's Illuminated Symphony

Tickled by the sun's warm grace,
Dancing shadows in a race.
Squirrels find their acorn stash,
Twirling tails, they make a splash.

Birds in chorus sing a tune,
Giggling clouds float past like balloons.
A fox in bow tie, oh what flair,
Prances through without a care.

Rabbits with their bunny hops,
Checking in at leafy shops.
With hats of grass and shoes of mud,
They prance around like it's a flood.

Thus, nature plays a silly game,
With wiggles, giggles, none the same.
Under the sun's bright, watching gaze,
We laugh at how the wild plays.

The Colorful Briefing of Winds

Watch the breezes hold a chat,
With whispers light as a fluffy cat.
They tickle trees and tease the vines,
Lifting spirits with playful signs.

A crow dons shades, feeling bold,
While butterflies flaunt hues of gold.
The chilly drafts giggle and quirk,
As flowers sway in a quirky smirk.

Bees in suits, buzzing their plan,
Promising sweet deals, oh what a span!
With dancing twirls that spin and glide,
Nature's commissions never hide.

Oh, the winds have quite a laugh,
In this vibrant, whimsical staff.
Nature's briefing? A cheeky sight,
As breezes giggle in sheer delight.

Elysian Glimmers Through the Woods

Sunbeams jiggle on leafy crowns,
While squirrels sport their fuzzy gowns.
A raccoon with a chef's tall hat,
Serves acorn soup, so fancy that!

Frogs croak jokes from lily pads,
While fireflies buzz, oh aren't they fads?
With winks and sparks that gleam and shine,
Lighting up the night like fine wine.

A hedgehog, dressed for a soirée,
Invites the owls, "Come out and play!"
With laughter echoing through the night,
Nature suggests, "Let's do it right!"

So dance in glimmers, join the fun,
Where woodland creatures are number one.
Under moonbeams, the night they roam,
In this glittering, wild, cozy home.

Harmonies of Nature's Palette

Brush strokes flutter across the land,
As critters with flair make a fun band.
Bashing on logs with sticks in tow,
The concert starts with a lively show.

Chirping crickets play the strings,
While cheerful robin happily sings.
Bees on tambourines, they thrive,
Creating buzz that feels so alive.

A deer with a crown of twigs so grand,
Leads the dance with a graceful stand.
With wildflowers chuckling in bloom,
They're painting joy, dispelling gloom.

So grab a seat on mossy ground,
As nature's palette spins around.
A symphonic laugh, oh what a spree,
In Mother Nature's revelry!

A Mosaic of Vibrant Moments

Colors splattered, what a sight,
A painter's dream in the morning bright.
Squirrels chase shadows, laugh and prance,
In a funny little game called 'Nature Dance.'

Sunbeams tickle the grass below,
While critters put on quite the show.
A ladybug hops, slips in the breeze,
With a tiny top hat, if you please!

Kisses of Afternoon Sun

Dandelion winks in the summer glow,
Sassy twirls, in the wind they flow.
A butterfly sneezes, flutters away,
As if to say, 'No pollen today!'

Grasshoppers boast, leaping with ease,
While ants are busy with their parties, tease.
'Hey Bob, where's the cake?' one shouts in fun,
'It's under my leaf, you'll have to run!'

The Lively Dance of Nature's Palette

Tulips gossip, their heads held high,
Chasing each other, you know why.
A breeze says, 'Tag! You're it, my dear!'
While daisies giggle from ear to ear.

The sun grins wide, playing peek-a-boo,
While clouds puff up, like popcorn too.
A robin struts, in a tutu quite rare,
Plays the lead in this vibrant affair!

Elements in a Brighter Shade

The wind whispers jokes, makes branches sway,
Who knew nature could be this cliché?
With hiccuping trees and chuckling vines,
It's a comedy show, oh how it shines!

Raindrops giggle as puddles leap,
A symphony of splashes, secrets to keep.
Frogs croak verses, the crickets applaud,
In this whimsical garden, funny and flawed!

A Journey Through Gilded Canopies

Beneath the trees, I skipped along,
Feeling like a weathered prong.
With squirrels planning their nutty heist,
I giggled at their furry feast, quite concise.

The sun peeked through with a cheeky grin,
As shadows played a game to win.
Each gust of wind was a breezy prank,
Whispering secrets from the leafy bank.

Branches waved like a dancing crew,
Inviting me to join their view.
I tripped on roots that seemed to gloat,
Like they were laughing at my clumsy tote.

In this place where bright colors collide,
Nature's jester plays with pride.
With a wink and a twist, I frolicked about,
In a world where laughter is never in doubt.

Nature's Brushstrokes in Dappled Light

The sun dripped down like spilled paint,
On branches that mimed a carefree saint.
I danced beneath the glittering show,
Where colors mixed in an artistic throw.

A bumblebee buzzed, a raucous tune,
Dropping its rhythm as if it were June.
I twirled around, thinking I could fly,
But tangled my feet, with a startled sigh.

The rustling vines joined in the fun,
Their whispers echoing, "Oh, we're not done!"
They formed a parade, all bright and neat,
As I found myself taking a comical seat.

In the Painted Place where chaos reigns,
Every stumble's a joy, nothing to feign.
With Nature's hand painting the air,
I laughed aloud, with not a single care.

The Radiance of What Remains

Once bright, the colors now grown old,
Swaying in winds, stories left untold.
Each shade a laugh, a memory's face,
I chuckled, convinced they won the race.

Golden whispers danced through the air,
As if nature's humor hid everywhere.
The ground was a canvas, quite messily spread,
With crunches beneath, like a giggle instead.

A butterfly flitted, a jester in flight,
Donning a costume, oh what a sight!
It dodged and dipped, like a slight-of-hand,
Making me smirk with its whimsical band.

In the glow of dusk, remnants take flight,
Each laugh from the past paints the night.
With remnants so vivid, they dance and twine,
In the radiance of what once did shine.

Stories Wrapped in Colorful Cloaks

Tales of tricksters wrapped up in hues,
Each shade a character, none meant to snooze.
With capes made of orange, gold, and green,
Their antics painted the air, quite the scene.

The wind croaked laughter, an old comedy show,
As branches shook hands with the ground below.
Every rustle was a giddy reply,
To the laughter that echoed, twirling up high.

A poet lost in the vibrant jest,
Worked hard to capture what nature expressed.
But with every giggle, each snort of delight,
The words took flight, escaping the night.

So here in this riot of color and fun,
I found stories blended, under the sun.
Each moment vivacious, each chuckle a cloak,
In the grand tale of life, laughter awoke.

Dance of the Dappled Canopy

In the breeze, they wiggle and sway,
Chasing shadows, come out to play.
A green ballet with no one to see,
Their twirls and flips, so wild and free.

With a giggle, they rustle so loud,
Challenging sunlight to draw a crowd.
They gossip of squirrels and acorn spies,
While the sun just chuckles and waves good-byes.

They wear coats of green and hints of gold,
In this leafy jest, they're brave and bold.
With every twist, they throw shade,
Oh, the stories these branches have made!

With each gust, they bring playful cheers,
Banishing gloom, chasing away fears.
Join the frolic, it's quite a sight,
In the dance that glimmers, beneath the light!

Radiant Rustle in Twilight

As dusk falls softly, they start to giggle,
In the twilight, they twist and wiggle.
Jokes about night and the moon's bright quirks,
Turn every branch into joyous jerks.

"Oh look, there goes a shadow man!
Quick, let's tickle him if we can!"
They snicker and shimmer, shaking with glee,
While the crickets join, a cacophony spree.

With each breeze that whispers, they clap with delight,
As fireflies join, lighting up the night.
They tell tales of adventures we never know,
Of what they heard, while so high they grow!

So come take a peek at their evening show,
Where jokes and laughter continue to flow.
In the splendid humor of night's gentle write,
These playful whispers, a warm, silly sight!

Veins of the Forest Floor

Underneath layers where secrets reside,
The roots have a party; they're ready to bide.
They share old gossip from trees up above,
Murmuring tales of old forest love.

"Oh, did you see how that oak stood tall?
Just last week, it tried to impress them all!"
They chuckle at ferns and their delicate selves,
Taking bets on which can dance off the shelves.

The soil is alive with laughter and cheer,
As critters run past, creeping near.
Every tiny pebble has stories to tell,
Of mischief and friendship in this earthy shell.

So join them below for a whimsical dance,
In the rich tapestry where roots take a chance.
They roll with the punches, stir up the lore,
Celebrating life from the forest's core!

Illumination Beneath the Boughs

In the quiet nook where shadows are bright,
Bright critters gather, all set for the night.
"Let's share our wisdom, take turns to boast,
I'll tell of the times I was scared of a ghost!"

"Were you speaking of that old tree's gnarled grin?
I swear I saw it wink at me while chowing in!"
The laughter erupts and echoes aloud,
Their chatter and banter—a comical crowd.

As each glimmering tale twirls in the air,
These whispers light up with a whimsical flair.
Bright fireflies capture the joyful intrigue,
Chasing the darkness away with intrigue.

So gather beneath where the fun never ends,
Join shadows and giggles, where humor transcends.
In the embrace of the boughs, we all find our place,
Where grins blossom wide like a jubilant face!

Chromatic Echoes in the Breeze

Colors twirl and swirl around,
Dancing softly, no sound found.
A cheeky breeze with playful cheer,
Steals my hat, oh dear, oh dear!

A yellow swirl starts to chase,
Slips and slides with such a grace.
Red joins in, a jolly sprint,
Whispers secrets, with a hint.

Tasks today? They fade away,
Chasing hues, I wish to stay.
The world's a collage, bright and bold,
Each tick of time feels uncontrolled.

Tiny critters join the race,
Scurrying with a silly face.
In this blend of color fun,
I laugh out loud, my heart's just won!

Fluttering Embraces of the Day

A flutter here, a giggle there,
Tiny joys dance in the air.
Daylight winks with a gleeful grin,
The silly chase is about to begin!

Bugs in bow ties, ants in a line,
Groovin' together, look so divine.
A ladybug slips, oh what a sight,
Rolling over, what a delight!

Sunshine's a jester, bright and warm,
Tickling branches, causing charm.
They saunter, they joke, like a flamboyant band,
Oops—a squirrel drops a nut, oh, how unplanned!

Time's a jester, playing tricks,
With every rustle, it deftly flicks.
Daring games of peek-a-boo,
Nature chuckles at me and you!

The Warmth Within the Grove

In a shady nook, with laughter bright,
The sun paints shadows, oh what a sight!
Critters plotting their silly schemes,
Whispering loudly, chasing dreams.

A rabbit pokes his ears out wide,
While a sly fox tries to hide.
Who knew being stealthy could be so grand,
As a ticklish breeze gives him a hand!

Chirps and giggles fill the trees,
Every crackle feels like tease.
A chubby squirrel spins with glee,
Climbing high, but oh so free!

Under branches, a party whirls,
Dances and twirls with flirty curls.
Lost in joy, in this cozy den,
Where sunlight tickles each playful friend.

Illuminated Patterns of Nature's Dance

Footloose figures twirl and glide,
Under the watch of the sun's bright ride.
Patterns shift, then spin with glee,
Oh, look—a snail goes for tea!

A wobbly mushroom starts to sway,
Begging for a dance today.
The wind snickers at the show,
As flickering shadows steal the glow.

Dandelions make a wish or two,
While acorns giggle, hiding from view.
Nature's brush paints with zest,
In this silly circus, we are blessed!

The sunlight spills like golden honey,
Tickling creatures, oh so funny.
Each leaf holds secrets, dreams, and prance,
In this riotous waltz, we all take a chance!

Foliage's Golden Glow

The greens and yellows start to dance,
The trees are in a bright romance.
With every gust, they swish and sway,
A leafy conga on display.

A squirrel's got a nut to share,
He twirls around without a care.
His acorn cap, a dapper hat,
As if he's practiced all of that.

Sunbeams tickle boughs above,
In every petal, there's a love.
The breeze, it giggles through each stem,
As if it knows the trees' great gem.

So here's to flora, bright and bold,
With stories whispering, never old.
In nature's laugh, they'll always live,
A funny show, they love to give.

The Serenade of Shimmering Branches

In twilight's glow, the branches hum,
While bugs in evening suits do strum.
They pull their strings, it feels so neat,
A playful tune from twig to sheet.

A rabbit taps his wiggly feet,
The rhythm's making him so fleet.
He jumps and spins, a furry star,
In nature's night, he's found his bar.

The owls hoot, they join the band,
With eerie notes—they lend a hand.
While crickets chirp their silly songs,
The forest joins, where fun belongs.

Each ripple through the rustling leaves,
Is laughter shared as twilight weaves.
This playful serenade takes flight,
As moonlight dances, oh what a sight!

Ribbons of Sunshine Through Verdant Halls

Sunshine streams like ribbons bright,
Through leafy tunnels, pure delight.
The colors burst in playful glee,
While squirrels play hide-and-seek with me.

A butterfly dons a polka dot dress,
Flitting about, it loves to impress.
It lands on noses, it's quite the show,
Leaving behind a hapless glow.

The grass beneath begins to twirl,
As giggling bunnies give a whirl.
They bounce around with cheerful shouts,
In this sunny game, there are no doubts.

These verdant halls hold secrets sweet,
Where nature's whimsy can't be beat.
With every turn, surprise is met,
In funky patches, no regret!

Capturing the Radiance of Change

A chameleon grins, oh what a sight,
His colors flip from day to night.
The shifting hues, a silly game,
He winks at shadows with no shame.

Windy whispers steal the show,
As mushrooms giggle in a row.
With every puff, they bounce around,
In their tiny tops, pure joy is found.

The daisies pop their heads up high,
With sunny faces, oh, my, oh my!
They chatter 'bout the funny change,
In hues and blooms, it's all so strange.

A bear in shades, just like a clown,
Stumbles forth, in nature's gown.
With every twist, a smile will bloom,
In seasons bright, let laughter loom!

The Tinctured Dance of Day

In the morning, colors splash,
Waking up the sleepy bash.
Sunshine tickles like a tease,
Whispering joy in every breeze.

Silly shadows start to play,
As the world begins its sway.
Colors twirl, a jolly sight,
Dancing in the warm daylight.

A butterfly, with wings so bright,
Flashes by, it's quite a sight!
With a wink, it zips away,
Making mischief, come what may.

Laughter echoes, nature's glee,
In this canvas, wild and free.
The tinctured dance, so absurd,
Who knew the sun could be so blurred?

Flickers of Joy on Breezy Trails

Dancing bugs in the warm sun,
Chasing shadows just for fun.
They zoom around, a merry crew,
Like little rockets, zipping through.

Squirrels mock in playful chatter,
While birds laugh in cheerful patter.
Each step's a giggle, a little tease,
Nature's whimsy finds its keys.

A hedgehog trips with a tiny squeak,
While flowers nod with a friendly peek.
Golden hues blend with a twist,
Who needs a map? Just follow bliss!

Whirlwind skirts of color float,
A flamboyant parade on every note.
Flickers of laughter in the air,
Every moment, without a care!

Amber Reflections in a Quiet Glade

Amidst the rustle of soft sounds,
A otter swims with grace that astounds.
Giggles ripple upon the stream,
Even trees join in, it seems!

Bright amber glimmers with a tease,
Finding fun in gentle breeze.
Bumblebees juggle flowers so sweet,
Nature's jesters, a comedic feat!

The brook sings tunes of pure delight,
While frogs leap in a playful fight.
Playtime here knows no bounds,
In this haven, joy surrounds.

Mushrooms sway in the shimmering glow,
Winking slyly, putting on a show.
Amber reflections, giggling trees,
This quiet glade is a laugh with ease!

Chasing Light Amongst the Canopy

Up above, the colors clash,
A rainbow fight with a boisterous splash.
Squirrels scamper with a wink,
While shadows hide, and giggles link.

Laughter bubbles from below,
As sunlight throws a playful glow.
The rustle tunes a silly song,
In the canopy, where all belong.

A parrot fluffs with a cheeky squawk,
While raccoons plot and gently stalk.
They chase the warmth; it's all a game,
In this wild world, none is the same.

In every hue, there's laughter bright,
A tapestry woven with sheer delight.
Chasing light amidst the trees,
Reveling in nature's goofy tease!

Warm Embrace of the Wind

The breeze tickled my nose, oh what a tease,
It danced with laughter through the trees.
Branches waved like they lost a bet,
Spinning tales that I'll never forget.

A squirrel sneezed, it's a furry affair,
Chasing its tail like it just doesn't care.
A bird laughed out loud, what a silly song,
Claiming it knew where the acorns belong.

Sunbeams tipped their hats, how very polite,
Casting shadows that played hide and seek, just right.
Nature's comedy, a sketch so absurd,
With giggles and whispers, not one word deterred.

Let's twirl around in this joyful chase,
Where gusts of whimsy leave no trace.
And when dusk descends, we'll burst into glee,
For tomorrow's antics, just wait and see!

Echoes of Vibrant Decay

In a rustling crowd, I heard a shout,
As wind whispered secrets, there's always a doubt.
A chipmunk dressed up, though it's not Halloween,
Strutting about in its vibrant sheen.

Rotting fruits held a grand parade,
With little bugs; oh what a charade!
They jived and they hopped on a squishy stage,
In this wild fest, I felt my age.

A twirling tumbleweed was quite the sight,
With a sassiness that sparked delight.
As petals giggled and dust bunnies swirled,
I chuckled along in this wacky world.

Each crackle and pop echoed through glee,
Even the compost joined in jubilee.
So let's toast to decay, quite a merry affair,
With nature's own humor, beyond compare!

Glistening Enchantment Above

Oh, how the sunlight loves to play,
Dancing off surfaces in a golden ballet.
Clouds fluff around like puffs of cream,
As I chase shadows, lost in the dream.

The raindrops trickle with a cheeky grin,
Joining the mischief's fun to begin.
A rainbow sneezed and sparked a delight,
Throwing colors like confetti in flight.

Twinkles above winking like stars,
Giggling at humans and their little cars.
In the vast ceiling, a fluffy white cat,
Curls up in the sun – imagine that!

Cactuses chuckle at how we wear hats,
While bees hum a tune that's awfully fat.
In this sparkly realm, joy overflows,
A melody of gibberish, but everyone knows!

Mosaics of Shimmering Colors

Puddles reflect a carnival bright,
With ducks in tuxedos ready to fight.
Each splash is a giggle, a pop of surprise,
As butterflies flutter with mischief in their eyes.

A kaleidoscope challenge, can you keep pace?
With swirling designs, we twist and we race.
Marigolds chatter about their new shoes,
While daisies gossip, gossiping news.

Crickets tap-dance in a chorus line,
Making the garden their stage divine.
Each hue a sharp joke, vibrant flair,
Laughter erupts on the breeze in the air.

So join the mosaic, come share in the fun,
As nature crafts beauty under the sun.
In the world of colors, merriment swirls,
A vibrant romance, take a twirl, give it a whirl!

Secrets Beneath the Arbor

Underneath the shady trees,
Squirrels conspire with the bees.
Whispers of acorns in a game,
Which one can find the biggest claim?

A secret stash, a merry song,
Everyone guffaws, 'What's that wrong?'
Roots gossip about the worms below,
Plotting pranks on the hawks in tow!

Mice dance in between the shoots,
Wearing little nutty boots.
The branches sway, a playful tease,
As if to say, 'Just chill, if you please!'

Laughter bubbles, hiding from sight,
Nature's jesters, what a delight!
Every rustle brings a cheer,
Under this tree, no worries here!

A Symphony of Sunlit Greens

In the glee of wiggle-waggle,
Caterpillars start to straggle.
Marching to a leafy tune,
Bouncing like a happy balloon!

Birds crack jokes about the cat,
As it slinks behind the mat.
'What do you call a feathery sight?
An avocado, feeling light!'

Breeze tickles the grass so bold,
'You're so sweet,' giggles the gold.
Chasing sunlight, we all sway,
Join the fun, and shout hooray!

Sunshine plays peekaboo,
With shadows that seem to coo.
Nature's laughter, pure and free,
A joyful dance, just you and me!

Glowing Embers of the Season

Autumn arrives with a playful frown,
Its colors turning the world upside down.
Pumpkin jokes are in the air,
Where's the scarecrow with colorful hair?

Charming winds whistle a silly song,
Rustling laughter, what could go wrong?
Acorns giggle as they fall,
Saying, 'Catch us, if you're small!'

Frogs in sweaters start to croak,
Laughing at the funny oak.
'That tree's a hoot,' one leaf will say,
'Look at its branches, what a display!'

During dusk, the sky glows red,
Nature's canvas blooms ahead.
Funny shapes dance with delight,
As day gives way to night!

Tapestry of Whispering Foliage

In the meadow where giggles sprout,
Flower pets gossip about the route.
Bumblebees share tales of flair,
'Have you seen my cousin's hair?'

The grass whispers to the old oak tree,
'Let's throw a party; our friends can be free!'
Joyful mice wheel in a line,
'The cheese is great, the drinks are fine!'

A waltzing breeze joins in the fun,
Stealing laughs from everyone.
Each branch sways with a wink and grin,
Nature's smile really draws us in!

Though seasons change, the fun remains,
In every rustle, there's no disdain.
A world of giggles, tales in the air,
Nature's humor, beyond compare!

Nature's Tapestry Unfurled

A squirrel in shades of brown,
Chasing shadows upside down.
It flips and hops with such great flair,
Wishing it had wings to dare.

The branches sway, they dance and twirl,
As critters scamper, spin, and whirl.
A funny breeze, it seems to tease,
Tickling all that rustle trees.

The sun peeks through, a golden hat,
To greet the critters as they chat.
The ants have meetings, oh what fun,
Arguing who has more snacks—none!

Nature's quilt, all stitched quite tight,
A patchwork woven, pure delight.
They giggle as the wind takes flight,
In this strange world of goofy sight.

Translucent Whispers of Green

A caterpillar, slow and wise,
Sips morning dew beneath the skies.
He's planning to soon have a change,
From munching greens to feeling strange.

The shadows stretch with playful glee,
As bunnies hop, delightfully free.
They dodge and weave from playful dogs,
While frogs lead limbs like jolly logs.

The sunlight pranks the twirling vines,
Telling jokes in fruity lines.
Each petal laughs, a colorful sight,
"Oh, watch me glow!" they tease with light.

The breezy sighs whisper around,
Confetti blooms fall to the ground.
Each swirling laugh fills up the scene,
In this madcap green machine.

Sun-Kissed Fragments Falling

A nut rolls down without a care,
But watch out! There's a squirrel there!
With cheeky eyes and twitchy tail,
He claims his prize without fail.

The sunbeams dance, they tickle toes,
As grass blinks shyly, then it grows.
The dandelions giggle bright,
Saying, "We're the stars tonight!"

Each fragment falls like laughter's sound,
A riot of colors all around.
The shadows hide, they know the score,
That nature's humor you can't ignore.

So come and play, let's skip and hop,
In nature's circus, we can't stop.
With every breeze, a fun-filled call,
Join us now, just have a ball!

Luminous Trails of the Season

In the forest, a game of hide,
Where butterflies zippity glide.
They giggle and share their silly tales,
While grasshoppers plot their hopping trails.

The groundhog peeks with a flirtatious grin,
He's got jokes under his chin.
As ladybugs laugh with tiny spots,
In this season's spotty plot.

Sunlight zips around like a bug,
Tickling petals with a happy hug.
Each tree sways like it knows the tune,
Throwing shade with a cheeky swoon.

Oh, the joy of this wild parade,
Where every moment is lovingly made.
Luminous trails, a sight to see,
In this wacky world of wild jubilee.

Enchanted Paths in Radiant Elegance

In the garden where shadows play,
The flowers giggle in bright array.
A clumsy bee trips on a petal,
As if it just found a new dance recital.

The sunbeams bounce like a bouncing ball,
While ants parade, oh they stand tall!
They march in line to a rhythm so loud,
Wishing for uniforms to make them proud.

The butterflies wear their finest attire,
As if they're heading to a fancy choir.
But oops! One slips and does a spin,
Landing right on a cheeky grin.

As laughter echoes through blooming bliss,
Nature's humor is hard to miss.
With every glance, a new sight to see,
In this whimsical world, so carefree!

Vibrant Whispers on the Wind

The breeze is tickling the daisies bright,
As they sway and giggle, what a sight!
A dandelion sneezes, scattering seeds,
Launching a frolic of whimsy and deeds.

Two squirrels argue over acorns so fine,
One pretends it's a diamond, oh what a line!
They leap and they bound, dramatic flair,
With such antics, it's hard not to stare.

A robin starts a solo in the tree,
While the cat nearby plots quietly.
"Is that a concert or a comedy show?"
The dog barks back, "I'm not sure, let's go!"

In this space of chatter and quirky delight,
Every breath of air fuels the night.
With giggles of critters, oh what a tease,
Nature's a stand-up, always sure to please!

A Dance of Colors Beneath the Skies

Radiant hues swirl like a wild dance,
While butterflies prance in a dizzying trance.
A ladybug slips on a curtain of gold,
With a flair like a star on stage, bold!

The sun winks at clouds, it's a playful plot,
While raindrops join in, quite the thought!
"Splash in puddles!" they blissfully shout,
As kids run with glee, giggling about.

A fox paints a masterpiece in the glen,
With strokes of mischief, again and again.
The trees laugh softly, "What a sly chap!"
As they watch all the colors, a topsy-turvy map!

Under skies like a jester's cap,
Nature's extravaganza, come take a nap.
With laughter and chaos, we take our part,
In this vibrant display that warms the heart!

Against the Glow of Dusk's Canvas

As dusk rolls in, colors change the show,
Crickets tune up for the evening's glow.
Fireflies bob like a funky parade,
While shadows giggle, unafraid.

The moon takes a sip from a silver cup,
While owls put on their wise guy makeup.
But a squirrel fluffs up, deciding to jest,
Saying, "I'm nocturnal; I'm the guest!"

A mist creeps in, making faces fun,
It plays peek-a-boo with everyone.
"Is that a sprite or just my old shoe?"
Echoes of laughter float through the blue.

In this gallery of twilight's delight,
Every flicker commands a giggle's flight.
With whispers of joy and mischief around,
Against this canvas, our fun knows no bounds!

Echoes of Life in Shimmering Shades

In the breeze, they dance and sway,
Wearing outfits of green all day.
Whispering secrets, gossiping loud,
Beneath the sun, they're such a crowd.

They tickle the toes of passerby,
While teasing squirrels as they fly.
With every rustle, a giggle's born,
Nature's jesters, never forlorn.

A fox overhears and starts to prance,
He tries to join their leafy dance.
But tripping over a root that's sly,
He lands in a pile of leaves with a sigh.

Yet still they cackle, light as air,
Mocking the fox without a care.
As day turns to night, their laughter stays,
In shimmering shades, they end their days.

The Artistry of Nature's Farewell

When autumn comes, they paint the ground,
With reds and golds, a sight profound.
They shrug off summer's heavy load,
And giggle down the winding road.

A painter calls with a careless brush,
While critters watch in a leafy hush.
The canvas grows, oh what a show!
Nature's palette, a vibrant glow.

Then off they flutter, a cheeky spree,
Whispering tales of wild jubilee.
They tickle the nose of every passer,
"Catch us if you can, you silly faster!"

As shadows stretch and daylight fades,
Their laughter lingers in gentle shades.
With every swirl that they create,
Nature laughs at the hands of fate.

Twilight's Embrace on Verdant Dreams

As dusk arrives, they start to twinkle,
Winking at stars with a playful sprinkle.
In whispers soft, they share their thoughts,
Of adventures grand and all they've sought.

A cricket sings to join the fun,
"Let's dance like we did under the sun!"
They sway in rhythm to a silent beat,
Nature's ballet, so light and sweet.

Chasing shadows, they spin around,
Telling tales of lost and found.
They weave through air, so full of cheer,
And laugh at the moon, "We'll see you here!"

With a twirl and a giggle, they bid goodnight,
Adventurous spirits, such pure delight.
In twilight's arms, they find their dreams,
With chuckles that echo in moonlit beams.

Celestial Patterns in Leafy Canopies

Up high they frolic, in shades so bold,
Mapping secrets that never grow old.
Like giggling friends, they chat and tease,
Hiding from winds with playful ease.

A woodpecker knocks with a rhythmic clang,
"Who can outsmart the tree's big tang?"
They rustle and wiggle in playful jest,
Nature's humor is always the best.

With the sun above and shadows below,
They play hide and seek, putting on a show.
As families stroll, they throw a laugh,
Creating a canopy, a leafy path.

And when the rain comes, they dance with glee,
Singing songs of joy from each tiny tree.
With droplets glistening, they take a bow,
In celestial patterns, laughing now.

Sunlit Treetop Murmurs

Up high above, a squirrel swings,
With comedy in all its flings.
A dance of branches, sways and hops,
As laughter echoes, never stops.

With sunlight dappling on its tail,
It plots its antics without fail.
A flip, a twist, then off it goes,
To find a nut, who really knows?

The chickadees join in the game,
With cheeky squawks, they'll stake their claim.
A feast of seeds they quirkily seek,
In this high place, they dance and squeak.

But watch out, folks, when gusts can blow,
Their feathery hijinks steal the show.
As branches bow with giggles bright,
Sunlit moments take their flight.

Dancing Shadows on the Forest Floor

A shadow waltzes, looking spry,
Turns out it's just a passing fly.
With stumbles and skips in fresh green hues,
This dance of critters comes with cues.

A rabbit bounds, its feet a blur,
While leaves above all jiggle and stir.
That shadow's split, it dodges light,
A game of hide-and-seek in flight.

Twirling spirits, what fun it breeds,
What's underneath? It's just some seeds.
They bounce and flounce, oh what a sight,
Nature's jesters in pure delight.

With every shift and playful tune,
A mighty chorus grows at noon.
They prance and play in glimmers bright,
The forest floor—a stage of light.

Amber Cradles of the Wind

In breezy arcs, they twirl and float,
Each golden piece, a tiny boat.
Caught on a gust, they skip and swirl,
In a dance as carefree as a girl.

They tumble down like silly jokes,
As if the trees just told some pokes.
With every rustle, a chuckle here,
They ride the breeze, without a fear.

Some land on noses, the pranksters' game,
While others join the whirlwind's fame.
A twinkling flutter starts to glide,
Spectrum of joy on every side.

In amber cradles, whispers cheer,
As breezes laugh from far and near.
These merry moments, so carefree,
In swirling warmth, it's jubilee.

Sun-Kissed Petals of Change

A flower opens, wide awake,
Silly petals start to shake.
With sunshine's tickle on its face,
It giggles soft, feels out of place.

The bees come buzzing, oh what fun,
They'll steal the show, just look and run.
With pollen jokes they're never shy,
Each bloom shakes head, "Just tell me why?"

And when the breeze brings chuckles near,
The petals grasp, then disappear.
The bloom may sigh, but don't you fret,
Next spring it'll be a bright vignette.

So laugh along with blossoms wild,
Nature's pranks make everyone a child.
For moments change, but joy remains,
In sun-kissed petals, life sustains.

www.ingramcontent.com/pod-product-compliance
Lightning Source LLC
Chambersburg PA
CBHW070317120526
44590CB00017B/2710